# PALEO BAKING

## Paleo Bread Recipes

# Table of Contents

Introduction
Old-Fashion Banana Bread
Cinnamon Raisin Bread
Italian Traditional Flatbread
Indian Naan
State Fair Fry Bread
Simple Paleo Pita
Strawberry Bread
Primal Apple Cider Buns
Pumpkin Coconut Bread
Green Bread
Paleo Cocoa Bread
Paleo Gingerbread
Curry Spice Bread
Banana Nut Bread
Paleo Egg Bread
Paleo Avocado Banana Bread
Primal Apple Bread
Savory Spiced Pineapple Bread
Primal Breakfast Buns
Cave Chicken Dumpling Bun

# Introduction

If you are new to the modern day caveman/woman eating plan, this is the book for you. The Paleo diet is based on the foods that our ancient ancestors ate up until 10,000 years ago. The theory goes that before the development of agriculture, which introduced wheat into the diet, the food selection was actually better suited for the human body's system. The diet includes fruits, vegetables, meat, seafood and nuts, which were all hunted and/or gathered. Now, modern day cavemen and women still have to hunt for these foods except instead of out in nature, it is in a sea of pre-packaged and processed foods. Studies have actually found a reduction in obesity, cardiovascular problems, type 2 diabetes complications and more when eating along Paleo guidelines. Big no-no's to the diet include any processed food, refined sugars, chemical additions or wheat-based products. Think all natural. There isn't a long list of foods to remember, all that needs to be asked is "Would a caveman have access to this?"

Many new Paleo eaters are wanting to start better eating habits. Some are wanting to lose weight, some may have health concerns they want to improve, but almost all Paleo eaters will have days they miss their beloved breads. Bread is a huge staple in the standard diet of almost every culture worldwide. The fact is: modern day bread, made from wheat, is really not beneficial for the body and its digestive tract. Paleo has a solution, and a delicious one at that! Try an assortment of Paleo approved recipes that look and taste like the bread favorites people know and love. Eat healthier ingredients and don't miss out on favorites like pancakes, dinner rolls and even cupcakes! Eating like a modern cavewoman isn't so hard with delicious recipes like these, not to mention the little conveniences like an oven in the kitchen. Enjoy baking delicious aromatic breads the Paleo way.

# Old-Fashion Banana Bread

Prep Time: 5 minutes

Cook Time: 25 minutes

Servings: 9

INGREDIENTS

3/4 cup almond flour

1/2 cup coconut flour

2 cage-free eggs

2 overripe bananas

1/4 sweetener*

2 tablespoons coconut oil

1 tablespoons baking powder

1 tablespoon cinnamon

1 teaspoon vanilla

1/2 teaspoon Celtic sea salt

2 firm bananas

4 dried pitted dates

1/4 cup water

INSTRUCTIONS

1. Preheat oven to 350 degrees F. Coat square baking pan with coconut oil or line with parchment.
2. Add pitted dates and water to food processor or bullet blender and process until dates are broken down.
3. Add processed dates to medium pan. Heat pan over medium-high heat.
4. Peel and chop firm bananas. Add to hot dates and sauté until caramelized, about 3 minutes. Remove from heat and set aside.
5. In medium mixing bowl, sift flour, baking powder, cinnamon, vanilla and salt.
6. Beat eggs, overripe bananas, coconut oil and sweetener in separate bowl with hand mixer or whisk. Add to flour mixture and mix to combine. Fold in candied bananas.
7. Pour batter into prepared baking pan and bake for about 25 minutes, or until browned and toothpick inserted into center comes out clean.
8. Let cool at least 5 minutes.
9. Slice and serve warm. Or allow to cool completely and serve room temperature.

NOTE: Bake in oiled loaf pan for about 40 minutes for **Old-Fashion Banana Bread** Loaf.

*stevia, raw honey or agave nectar

# Cinnamon Raisin Bread

Prep Time: 5 minutes

Cook Time: 20 minutes

Servings: 12

INGREDIENTS

3/4 cup coconut flour

3/4 cup almond flour

1/4 cup ground chia seed (or flax meal)

2 cage-free eggs

1/2 cup raisins

1/2 cup coconut oil

1/2 cup unsweetened applesauce

1/4 cup sweetener*

2 tablespoons ground cinnamon

1 teaspoon baking powder

1 teaspoon Celtic sea salt

1/2 teaspoon ground black pepper (optional)

## INSTRUCTIONS

1. Preheat oven to 350 degrees F.  Line baking pan with parchment or coat with coconut oil.
2. In large bowl, whisk eggs with hand mixer or whisk until frothy and light. Add coconut oil, sweetener and applesauce. Blend until combined.
3. Sift coconut and almond flour, chia meal, baking powder, salt and spices into wet ingredients. Beat until smooth and well combined. Stir in raisins.
4. Pour batter into prepared baking pan.
5. Bake for 20 - 25 minutes, or until golden brown and firm to the touch.
6. Remove from oven and let cool about 5 minutes.
7. Slice and serve warm. Or allow to cool completely and serve room temperature.

NOTE: Bake in oiled loaf pan for 40 - 45 minutes for **Cinnamon Raisin Bread** loaf.

*stevia, raw honey or agave nectar*

# Italian Traditional Flatbread

Prep Time: 10 minutes

Cook Time: 15 minutes

Servings: 4

INGREDIENTS

1 cup coconut flour

1/2 cup tapioca flour

1/4 cup chia seed meal (or flax meal)

2 cage-free eggs

3/4 cup water

1 teaspoon baking powder

1 teaspoon dried basil

1 teaspoon dried oregano

1/2 teaspoon ground black pepper

1/2 teaspoon Celtic sea salt

## INSTRUCTIONS

1. Preheat oven to 350 degrees F. Line sheet pan with parchment paper. Prepare two additional sheets of parchment paper.

2. Whisk eggs and water in medium bowl. Set aside.

3. Combine flours, chia meal, baking powder and salt in medium bowl.

4. Pour egg mixture into flour mixture, plus spices. Mix well until dough pulls together. If dough is sticky, add 1 tablespoon of coconut flour at a time to reach proper consistency.

5. Flatten dough into basic square shape with hands on one sheet of parchment on cutting board. Cover with second sheet and use rolling pin flatten dough to about 1/8 inch thick rectangle.

6. Cut flatbread dough with pizza cutter or sharp knife into four equal pieces.

7. Gently remove top used parchment sheet and replace with fresh sheet from sheet pan. Invert sheet pan over dough and flip cutting board and sheet pan over. Replace cutting board and gently remove top used parchment sheet.

8. Use spatula to separate flatbreads. Bake in oven for 12 -15 minutes, until browned and firm. Cool and serve.

NOTE: For crisper **Flatbread**, fry flattened dough segments in oiled skillet over medium heat for about 3 minutes on each side, until puffed and browned.

# Indian Naan

Prep Time: 5 minutes

Cook Time: 15 minutes

Servings: 4

INGREDIENTS

1/2 cup coconut flour

4 cage-free eggs

1/4 cup coconut oil

1/2 - 2/3 cup water

1/4 tsp baking powder

1/2 teaspoons Celtic sea salt

Coconut oil (for cooking)

INSTRUCTIONS

1.  Heat medium skillet over medium-high heat and coat generously with coconut oil.
2.  Blend flour, eggs, oil, baking powder, salt and 1/2 cup water in a food processor or bullet blender. Process until smooth. Add liquid if batter is too thick, and coconut flour if too thin. You want a moderately thin batter.
3.  Pour 1/4$^{th}$ of batter into hot oiled skillet. Cook until naan bubbles and browns, about 2 minutes. Then flip and cook another 2 minutes, or until golden and firm.
4.  Repeat with remaining batter. Re-oil pan as necessary.
5.  Drain hot naan on paper towel. Serve warm.

NOTE: For softer **Baked Naan** , bake at 425 degrees F in two (2 )9-inch round cake pans generously coated with coconut oil for 10 minutes, or until cooked through.

# State Fair Fry Bread

Prep Time: 5 minutes

Cook Time: 15 minutes

Servings: 2

INGREDIENTS

1 cup coconut flour

1 cup almond flour (or cashew flour)

1/4 cup tapioca flour/starch

3 cage-free eggs

1/2 cup coconut oil

1/2 cup full-fat coconut milk

1 teaspoon baking powder

2 tablespoons sweetener*

Pinch Celtic sea salt

Water (for thinning)

Coconut oil (for cooking)

## INSTRUCTIONS

1. Heat medium skillet over medium-high heat and coat generously with coconut oil.
2. Blend eggs, oil, milk and sweetener in food processor or bullet blender until smooth and a bit airy.
3. In medium bowl, combine flours, baking powder and salt. Add egg mixture and combine to form soft dough. If too tough, add water 1 tablespoon at a time.
4. Form dough into 2 large flat rounds with hands. Place 1 round in pan and cook about 3 minutes, or until puffed and browned. Flip fry bread with tongs or spatula and cook another 3 minutes, or until golden and cooked through.
5. Repeat with remaining dough. Re-oil pan as necessary.
6. Drain hot fry bread on paper towel. Serve warm.

NOTE: For **Baked Fry Bread** , generously coat two 9-inch round cake pans with coconut oil. Press dough into pans  and brush tops with coconut oil. Bake at 425 degrees F in  for 15 minutes, or until cooked through and golden.

*stevia, raw honey or agave nectar

# Simple Paleo Pita

Prep Time: 5 minutes

Cook Time: 20 minutes

Servings: 1

INGREDIENTS

1 cup tapioca flour/starch

1 cage-free egg

2 tablespoons coconut oil (or almond oil)

1 teaspoon ground chia seed (flax meal)

5 tablespoons water

1/2 teaspoon baking soda

1/4 teaspoon Celtic sea salt

INSTRUCTIONS

1.  Preheat oven to 375 degrees F. Cover sheet pan with parchment
    paper. Heat small pot over low heat.

2. Mix 1/3 cup flour, chia meal, water and 1 tablespoon oil in pan. Stir until mixture comes together. Remove from heat and cool in freezer.

3. In medium bowl, blend remaining flour, baking soda and salt. Then add egg and remaining oil. Mix until combined .

4. Add cooled chia mixture to bowl. Mix to combine, then remove and knead to form dough.

5. Form round disk, then flatten on baking sheet lined with parchment.

6. Bake about 15 minutes. Carefully turn over with spatula and bake another 5 - 10 minutes, or until crisp.

7. Remove from oven and cut into wedges. Serve warm or cooled.

NOTE: For **Pita Chips** , place baked wedges on oiled sheet pan, brush tops with coconut oil and broil in oven for about 2 minutes on each side. *Watch carefully and do not burn!*

# Strawberry Bread

Prep Time: 10 minutes

Cook Time: 10 minutes

Servings: 12 - 16

INGREDIENTS

1 cup coconut flour

3/4 cup cashew flour (or almond flour)

1/4 cup ground chia seed (or flax meal)

1/2 cup coconut oil

2 cage-free eggs

1/4 cup coconut crème

1/4 cup sweetener*

1/4 cup unsweetened apple sauce

1 teaspoons baking powder

1 tablespoon ground cinnamon

1 teaspoon ground ginger

1 teaspoon ground white pepper (or black pepper)

1 teaspoon Celtic sea salt

2 cups fresh sliced strawberries

1/2 cup chopped walnuts (optional)

## INSTRUCTIONS

1. Preheat oven to 350 degrees F. Line muffin pan with paper liners or coat with coconut oil.

2. In large bowl, whisk eggs with hand mixer or whisk until frothy and light. Add coconut oil, sweetener and applesauce. Blend until combined. Slice strawberries, and fold in with walnuts (optional).

3. In medium bowl, blend flours, chia meal, baking powder, salt and spices. Stir flour blend into strawberry mixture until well combined.

4. Use ice cream scoop or tablespoon to scoop equal portions of batter into muffin pans, 1/2 - 3/4 full. Line or oil more muffin pans if excess batter remains.

5. Bake for 15 minutes, or until golden brown and firm but springy to the touch.

6. Cool enough to handle. Serve warm or room temperature.

NOTE: Bake in square oiled baking pan for 25 - 35 minutes or two oiled loaf pans for 35 - 45 minutes for **Strawberry Loaves**.

*stevia, raw honey or agave nectar*

# Primal Apple Cider Buns

Prep Time: 10 minutes

Cook Time: 20 minutes

Servings: 24

INGREDIENTS

2 cups coconut flour

1 cup almond flour

12 ounces organic hard cider

2 cage-free eggs

1/2 cup unsweetened applesauce

1 tart apple

2 tablespoons baking powder

1 teaspoon ground nutmeg

1 teaspoon ground black pepper

1 teaspoon Celtic sea salt

# INSTRUCTIONS

1. Preheat oven to 375 degrees F. Line 2 muffin pans with paper liners or coat with coconut oil.

2. Peel, core and grate or dice apple, and place in large bowl. Pour hard apple cider over apples, plus nutmeg and black pepper.

3. In medium bowl, whisk eggs with hand mixer or whisk until frothy and light. Add applesauce and blend until combined. Add egg mixture to cider and apples.

4. Slowly sift and stir flours, baking powder and salt into wet ingredients.

5. Use ice cream scoop or tablespoon to scoop equal portions of batter into muffin pans, 1/2 - 3/4 full.

6. Bake for 15 - 20 minutes, or until golden brown and firm but springy to the touch.

7. Cool enough to handle. Serve warm or room temperature.

NOTE: Bake in square oiled baking pan for 35 - 45 minutes or two oiled loaf pans for 45 - 55 minutes for **Primal Apple Cider Loaves**.

*stevia, raw honey or agave nectar*

# Pumpkin Coconut Bread

Prep Time: 5 minutes

Cook Time: 25 minutes

Servings: 12

INGREDIENTS

1 3/4 cups coconut flour

2 cage-free eggs

1/4 cup coconut oil

1/2 cup coconut milk

1/2 unsweetened applesauce

1/4 cup sweetener*

15 oz (1 can) pumpkin puree

2 teaspoons baking soda

1 tablespoon ground cinnamon

1 teaspoon ground nutmeg

1 teaspoon Celtic sea salt

1/2 cup flaked coconut

1/4 cup pumpkin seeds

Water

## INSTRUCTIONS

1. Preheat oven to 350 degrees F. Coat square baking pan with coconut oil.

2. Process eggs, coconut oil, coconut milk, applesauce and sweetener in food processor or blender until thick and lightened. Pour into medium mixing bowl. Mix in pumpkin puree and spices.

3. Mix in flour, baking soda, flaked coconut and pumpkin seeds. Stir until combined.

4. Pour batter into oiled baking pan. Bake 20 - 25 minutes, or until firm but springy in center.

5. Serve warm or room temperature.

NOTE: Bake in lined or oiled muffin pan for 15 - 20 minutes for **Pumpkin Coconut Muffins**.

*stevia, raw honey or agave nectar*

# Green Bread

Prep Time: 5 minutes

Cook Time: 20 minutes

Servings: 12

INGREDIENTS

1 3/4 cups almond flour

1/4 cup flax seed meal (or ground chia seed)

3 cage-free eggs

3 avocados

1/2 cup unsweetened applesauce (or apple butter)

1/4 cup sweetener*

1/2 cup fresh squeezed orange juice

1 tablespoon orange zest

1 tablespoon baking powder

1 teaspoon ground cinnamon

1 teaspoon ground allspice

1 teaspoon ground black pepper

1 teaspoon Celtic sea salt

## INSTRUCTIONS

1. Preheat oven to 350 degrees F. Coat square baking pan with coconut oil.

2. Slice avocados in half, pit, and scoop flesh into food processor or blender. Add eggs, applesauce, sweetener and orange juice and blend until smooth.

3. Pour avocado blend into medium mixing bowl. Stir in almond flour, flax meal, baking powder, salt, orange zest and spices until combined.

4. Pour batter into oiled baking pan. Bake 20 - 25 minutes, or until firm but springy in center.

5. Serve warm or room temperature.

NOTE: Bake in lined or oiled muffin pan for 15 - 20 minutes for **Green Spice Muffins**.

*stevia, raw honey or agave nectar*

# Paleo Cocoa Bread

Prep Time: 10 minutes

Cook Time: 20 minutes

Servings: 8

INGREDIENTS

1 cup coconut flour

6 cage-free eggs

1/2 cup unsweetened applesauce

1/4 cup coconut milk

1/2 teaspoon baking soda

2 tablespoons raw cocoa powder

1/2 teaspoon ground black pepper

1/2 teaspoon salt

INSTRUCTIONS

1. Preheat oven to 350 degrees F. Coat 2 small loaf pans with coconut oil.
2. Separate eggs. In large bowl, whisk egg whites to soft peaks with hand mixer or whisk. Add yolks, applesauce and coconut milk. Mix until combined.
3. Sift in flour, baking soda, cocoa powder, black pepper and salt. Stir to combine.
4. Pour batter into oiled loaf pans. Bake 20 - 25 minutes, or until firm but springy in center.
5. Serve warm or room temperature.

NOTE: Bake in large oiled loaf pan for 30 - 40 minutes for **Paleo Cocoa Loaf**.

# Paleo Gingerbread

Prep Time: 5 minutes

Cook Time: 20 minutes

Servings: 8

INGREDIENTS

2 cups almond flour

2 tablespoons ground chia seed (or flax meal)

2 cage-free eggs

1/2 cup unsweetened applesauce

1/4 cup coconut oil

1/4 cup sweetener*

1 tablespoon baking powder

1 teaspoon baking soda

2 tablespoons ground ginger

1 tablespoon vanilla

1 tablespoon ground cinnamon

1 teaspoon ground black pepper

1/2 teaspoon ground cloves

1/2 teaspoon cardamom (optional)

1 oz fresh ginger juice (optional)

## INSTRUCTIONS

1. Preheat oven to 350 degrees F. Coat 2 small loaf pans with coconut oil.

2. In large bowl, beat eggs until light and thickened. Add applesauce, oil, sweetener and ginger juice (optional). Beat well.

3. In medium bowl, blend all dry ingredients well. Slowly stir flour mixture into egg mixture.

4. Pour batter into loaf pans and bake for 20 - 25 minutes, or until toothpick inserted into center comes out clean.

5. Let cool slightly. Insert knife around edges and remove from pan. Serve warm or room temperature.

NOTE: Bake in large oiled loaf pan for 35 - 45 minutes for **Paleo Gingerbread Loaf**.

*raw honey, agave nectar, grade B maple syrup, molasses*

# Curry Spice Bread

Prep Time: 5 minutes

Cook Time: 20 minutes

Servings: 8

INGREDIENTS

2 cups almond flour

2 cage-free eggs

1/2 cup unsweetened applesauce

1/4 cup coconut oil

Juice of 1 lemon

Juice of 1 orange

1 teaspoon lemon zest

1 teaspoon orange zest

1 tablespoon apple cider vinegar

2 tablespoons baking powder

1 tablespoon vanilla

1 tablespoon curry powder

1 teaspoon ground cinnamon

1 teaspoon ground ginger

1 teaspoon ground white pepper (or black pepper)

1 teaspoon cardamom (optional)

1/ 4 cup pumpkin seeds (optional)

Pinch Celtic sea salt

## INSTRUCTIONS

1. Preheat oven to 350 degrees F. Coat 2 small loaf pans with coconut oil.

2. Separate eggs. In large bowl, whisk egg whites to soft peaks with hand mixer or whisk. Add yolks, applesauce, oil, juices, zests and vinegar. Beat well.

3. In medium bowl, blend flour, baking powder, spices and salt. Stir flour mixture into egg mixture.

4. Pour batter into loaf pans and bake for 20 - 25 minutes, or until toothpick inserted into center comes out clean.

5. Let cool slightly. Insert knife around edges and remove from pan. Serve warm or room temperature.

NOTE: Bake in large oiled loaf pan for 35 - 45 minutes for **Curry Spice Loaf**.

*stevia, raw honey or agave nectar*

# Banana Nut Bread

Prep Time: 5 minutes

Cook Time: 20 minutes

Servings: 9

INGREDIENTS

3/4 cup of almond flour

1/4 cup of coconut flour

2 tablespoons flax meal (or ground chia seed)

2 cage-free eggs

2 overripe bananas

1/4 sweetener*

2 tablespoons coconut oil

1/4 cup walnuts

1/4 cup hazelnuts

1 tablespoon baking powder

1 tablespoon cinnamon

1 teaspoon nutmeg

1 teaspoon vanilla

1/2 teaspoon Celtic sea salt

## INSTRUCTIONS

1. Preheat oven to 350 degrees F. Coat square baking pan with coconut oil.
2. In medium bowl, beat eggs, bananas, oil, flax or chia, and sweetener.
3. In separate bowl, blend flour, baking powder, salt and spices. Pour banana mixture in flour mixture and blend. Fold in nuts.
4. Pour batter into baking pan and bake for 20 - 25 minutes, or until browned and firm in the center.
5. Let cool slightly. Serve warm or room temperature.

NOTE: Bake in oiled loaf pan for 35 - 45 minutes for **Banana Nut Loaf**.

*stevia, raw honey or agave nectar*

# Paleo Egg Bread

Prep Time: 15 minutes

Cook Time: 20 minutes

Servings: 4

INGREDIENTS

3 cups almond flour

6 cage-free egg yolks (room temperature)

3 cage-free eggs (room temperature)

1/2 cup coconut oil

1/4 cup sweetener*

1 tablespoon apple cider vinegar

1 teaspoon baking soda

1/2 teaspoon  Celtic sea salt

1 cage-free egg

INSTRUCTIONS

1. Preheat oven to 350 degrees F. Coat muffin pan with coconut oil or line with paper liners. Cover cutting board with parchment.

2. Add eggs and yolks to large mixing bowl. Beat with hand mixer or whisk until light and frothy. Beat in coconut oil, sweetener, vinegar, baking soda and salt. Sift in 2 1/2 cups almond flower while mixing to form sticky dough.

3. Dust parchment covered cutting board with remaining almond flour. Turn dough out onto parchment and knead for about 5 minutes.

4. Transfer dough to prepared muffin pan. Beat remaining egg in small mixing bowl and brush over bread.

5. Place in oven and bake 15 - 20 minutes, until browned and cooked through.

6. Remove from oven and let cool for 5 minutes.

7. Serve warm. Or allow to cool completely and serve room temperature.

*\* stevia, raw honey or agave nectar*

NOTE: Bake in oiled loaf pan for 40 minutes for **Egg Bread Loaf**, or form ropes and braid dough together then bake on prepared sheet pan for 30 minutes for **Classic Egg Bread**.

# Paleo Avocado Banana Bread

Prep Time: 5 minutes

Cook Time: 25 minutes

Servings: 9

INGREDIENTS

3/4 cup almond flour

1/4 cup coconut flour

2 tablespoons flax meal (or ground chia seed)

2 cage-free eggs

1 large overripe banana

1 avocado

1/4 cup sweetener*

2 tablespoons coconut oil

1 tablespoon baking powder

1 tablespoon cinnamon

1 teaspoon ground ginger

1 teaspoon vanilla

1/2 teaspoon ground black pepper

1/2 teaspoon Celtic sea salt

1/2 cup organic banana chips (optional)

## INSTRUCTIONS

1. Preheat oven to 350 degrees F. Coat square baking pan with coconut oil.
2. Slice avocado in half. Remove pit and scoop flesh into medium mixing bowl. Peel banana and add to bowl with eggs, sweetener, and flax or chia meal. Beat with hand mixer or whisk until well blended.
3. Sift flour, baking powder, salt and spices Into banana mixture. Mix until combined. Roughly chop banana chips and fold into batter (optional).
4. Pour batter into baking pan and bake for 20 - 25 minutes, or until browned and firm in the center.
5. Remove from oven and let cool at least 5 minutes.
6. Slice and serve warm. Or allow to cool completely and serve room temperature.

NOTE: Bake in oiled loaf pan for 35 - 45 minutes for **Avocado Banana Loaf**.

*stevia, raw honey or agave nectar*

# Primal Apple Bread

Prep Time: 10 minutes

Cook Time: 20 minutes

Servings: 24

INGREDIENTS

2 cups coconut flour

1 cup almond flour

2 tablespoons tapioca flour (or arrowroot powder)

2 cage-free eggs

1 tart apple

1 sweet apple

1/2 cup unsweetened applesauce

1/4 cup coconut oil

1/4 cup sweetener*

1 tablespoon baking soda

1 tablespoon apple cider vinegar

1 teaspoon ground cinnamon

1 teaspoon ground ginger

1 teaspoon Celtic sea salt

1/2 teaspoon ground white  pepper (or ground black pepper)

## INSTRUCTIONS

1. Preheat oven to 375 degrees F.  Line 2 muffin pans with paper liners or coat with coconut oil.

2. Peel, core and grate or dice apples, and place in small bowl. Pour vinegar and spices over apples. Toss to coat.

3. In medium bowl, whisk eggs with hand mixer or whisk until light and thickened, about 2 minutes. Add applesauce, sweetener and coconut oil. Blend until combined. Mix in apples.

4. Sift flours, baking soda and salt into apple mixture and mix until combined.

5. Use ice cream scoop or tablespoon to scoop equal portions of batter into muffin pans until 2/3 - 3/4 full.

6. Place in oven and bake for 15 - 20 minutes, or until golden brown and firm but springy to the touch.

7. Remove form oven and let cool at least 5 minutes.

8. Serve warm/ Or allow to cool completely and serve room temperature.

NOTE: Bake in oiled square baking pan for 35 - 45 minutes or two loaf pans for 45 - 55 minutes for **Primal Apple Bread Loaves**.

# Savory Spiced Pineapple Bread

Prep Time: 5 minutes

Cook Time: 20 minutes

Servings: 8

INGREDIENTS

2 cups almond flour

3 cage-free eggs

1/4 cup coconut oil

1 cup crushed pineapple (canned in juice or fresh)

1 tablespoon apple cider vinegar

2 teaspoons baking soda

2 teaspoons vanilla

2 teaspoons ground cinnamon

2 teaspoons ground ginger

1/2 teaspoon ground nutmeg

1/2 teaspoon paprika

1/2 teaspoon cayenne pepper

1 teaspoon ground white pepper (or black pepper)

1 teaspoon Celtic sea salt

1 teaspoon cardamom (optional)

1 teaspoon turmeric (optional)

## INSTRUCTIONS

1. Preheat oven to 350 degrees F.  Coat 2 small loaf pans with coconut oil.
2. Separate eggs. In large bowl, beats egg whites to soft peaks with hand mixer or whisk, about 5 minutes.  Add yolks, crushed or blended pineapple, coconut oil and vinegar. Beat well.
3. In medium bowl, blend flour, baking soda, spices and salt. Pour flour mixture into egg mixture and mix well.
4. Pour batter into loaf pans and bake for about 25 minutes, until toothpick inserted into center comes out clean.
5. Remove oven and let cool at least 5 minutes. Insert knife around edges and remove from pan.
6. Slice and serve warm. Or let cool completely and serve room temperature.

NOTE: Bake in large oiled loaf pan for 35 - 45 minutes for **Savory Spiced Pineapple Loaf**.

# Primal Breakfast Buns

Prep Time: 15 minutes

Cook Time: 20 minutes

Servings: 4

INGREDIENTS

*Breakfast Bun*

1 cup tapioca flour

1/4 - 1/3 cup coconut flour

1 cage-free egg

1/2 cup warm water

1/4 cup coconut oil

Bacon drippings

2 tablespoons applesauce

1 teaspoon apple cider vinegar

1/2 teaspoon baking soda

1/2 teaspoon ground black pepper

1/4 teaspoon Celtic sea salt

*Filling*

4 cage-free eggs

4 slices nitrate-free bacon

1/2 small bell pepper

1/2 small onion

1/4 teaspoon ground black pepper

1/4 teaspoon Celtic sea salt

## INSTRUCTIONS

1. Preheat oven to 350 degrees F. Line sheet pan with parchment paper or coat with coconut oil. Heat medium skillet over medium-high heat. Add water to small pot and heat over medium heat.

2. For *Filling*, peel onion, stem, seed and vein pepper, and chop bacon. Add bacon to hot skillet and sauté until bacon is crisp and almost cooked through. Drain off drippings and set aside.

3. Dice onion and pepper and add to bacon. Sauté about 2 minutes, unto bacon is cooked through and veggies are softened. Add eggs and lightly scrambled, just 30 seconds - 1 minute. Remove from heat and set aside.

4. For *Breakfast Bun*, sift together tapioca flour, coconut flour, baking soda, salt and pepper in medium bowl.

5. Whisk egg, applesauce and vinegar in small bowl. Whisk in warm water, coconut oil and bacon drippings.

6. Add egg mixture to flour mixture and mix until well combined. Add 1 tablespoon coconut flour or water at a time if needed to form soft and slightly sticky dough.

7. Divide dough into 4 portions and flatten into round disks. Dust your hand or rolling pin with extra tapioca flour to prevent sticking.

8. Scoop loose egg *Filling* into center of each dough disk and pinch edges of dough together to create round, sealed ball.

9. Place filled buns sealed side down on sheet pan and pat down slightly.

10. Place in oven and bake 20 minutes, or until edges are golden brown and dough is cooked through.

11. Remove from oven and let cool about 5 minutes.

12. Serve warm.

# Cave Chicken Dumpling Bun

Prep Time: 15 minutes

Cook Time: 20 minutes

Servings: 4

INGREDIENTS

*Dumpling Bun*

1 cup tapioca flour

1/4 - 1/3 cup coconut flour

1 cage-free egg

1/2 cup warm chicken stock

1/4 cup coconut oil

1/4 cup applesauce

1 teaspoon apple cider vinegar

1 teaspoon baking soda

1/2 teaspoon onion powder

1/ 4 teaspoon garlic powder

1/2 teaspoon Celtic sea salt

*Filling*

8 oz boneless chicken (breasts, thighs, etc.)

1 small carrot

1 small celery stalk

1/2 teaspoon dried thyme

1/4 teaspoon ground sage

1/2 teaspoon ground black pepper

1/2 teaspoon Celtic sea salt

# INSTRUCTIONS

1. Preheat oven to 350 degrees F. Line sheet pan with parchment paper or coat with coconut oil. Heat medium skillet over medium heat and lightly coat with coconut oil.

2. Add chicken stock to small pot and heat over medium heat.

3. For *Filling*, dice carrot and celery, fillet chicken in half, and add to hot oiled skillet with salt and spices. Sauté until chicken is cooked through and browned and veggies are softened, about 5 - 8 minutes. Remove from heat and set aside. Shred or dice rested chicken and mix thoroughly with sautéed veggies.

4. For *Dumpling Bun*, sift together tapioca flour, coconut flour, baking soda, salt and spices in medium bowl.

5. Whisk egg, applesauce and vinegar in small bowl. Whisk in warm chicken stock and coconut oil.

6.  Add egg mixture to flour mixture and mix until well combined. Add 1 tablespoon coconut flour or water at a time if needed to form soft and slightly sticky dough.

7.  Divide dough into 4 portions and flatten into round disks. Dust your hand or rolling pin with extra tapioca flour to prevent sticking.

8.  Scoop chicken *Filling* into center of each dough disk and pinch edges of dough together to create round, sealed ball.

9.  Place filled buns sealed side down on sheet pan and pat down slightly.

10. Place in oven and bake 20 minutes, or until edges are golden brown and dough is cooked through.

11. Remove from oven and let cool about 5 minutes.

12. Serve warm.